The Walter Lynwood Fleming
Lectures in Southern History
Louisiana State University

THE PERSISTENT TRADITION
IN NEW SOUTH POLITICS

THE PERSISTENT
TRADITION IN
NEW SOUTH POLITICS

GEORGE BROWN TINDALL

LOUISIANA STATE UNIVERSITY PRESS
BATON ROUGE

ISBN 0–8071–0098–6
Library of Congress Catalog Card Number 74–27194
Copyright © 1975 by Louisiana State University Press
All rights reserved
Manufactured in the United States of America
Designed by Dwight Agner
Printed by Moran Industries, Inc., Baton Rouge, Louisiana

Publication of this book was assisted by the
LSU Athletic Council through a grant to
the Council on Research.

To my mother and father
NELLIE BROWN TINDALL
GOIN ROSCOE TINDALL

CONTENTS

PREFACE

W HEN THE invitation to prepare these lectures came, I was revising for publication another triad of lectures delivered at Mercer University and entitled *The Disruption of the Solid South*. It occurred to me that, having just pursued the decline and fall of the Solid South, I might seize the opportunity for a fresh look at the old regime, now ended.

One thing that drew me on was a striking durability in the nomenclature of southern politics, despite all the change that had occurred. Three significant episodes and groups had dominated the story of post-Reconstruction politics: Bourbons, Populists, and Progressives. And the pundits of the 1970s were still finding Bourbons, Populists, and Progressives on the current scene. Thomas B. Alexander had written of "persistent Whigs" in the Confederate and postbellum South. Were there perhaps also persistent Bourbons, Populists, and Progressives in the twentieth century?

As the writing progressed, however, a different frame of reference began to emerge. The first step was to place each of the groups in historiographical perspective, to see how interpretations had grown and changed over the years. Out of that review the notion gradually emerged that a thread of continuity ran through the transition from Bourbonism to progressivism in the New South. One might argue, without advancing the point as dogma, that a process of dialectic had occurred. The Bourbons supplied a thesis, the Populists set up an antithesis, and the Progressives worked out a synthesis which governed southern politics through the first half of the twentieth century.

The Bourbons had achieved the ultimate success of all durable conservative movements, the reconciliation of tradition with innovation. While inventing a New South they kept alive the vision of a traditional organic community. The Populists challenged that vision, or so at least the Bourbons thought, and thus had to be put down by fair means or foul. The Progressives, finally, while they took over certain "populistic" ideas of a more active government, were the legitimate heirs of the Bourbons. Built into their synthesis was the persistent tradition of community in the South.

This, in short, is the central theme of these lectures. No

implication is made or intended, however, that it is the central theme of southern political history, nor that it will resolve the complexities of the subject.

Presenting the Fleming Lectures in the spring of 1973 gave me an opportunity for a nostalgic return to the campus of Louisiana State University, to which I had come twenty years before as a junior professor. My visit was cheered by the hospitality of two former colleagues, John Loos and Robert Holtman, and their wives, Helen and Wilbur. It was reassuring to find that LSU's history department still maintains its persistent tradition of high-toned banter and the instant retort.

The second of these essays leans heavily upon an article, "Populism: A Semantic Identity Crisis," published in the *Virginia Quarterly Review*, XLVIII (Autumn, 1972), 501–518; and the third draws some material from *The Emergence of the New South, 1913–1945* (Baton Rouge: Louisiana State University Press, 1967). In revised form the first and third lectures were given as the Ralph Brown Draughon Lectures at Auburn University on November 14–15, 1974.

I am grateful to Linda Price for typing the lectures twice, the first time on a rush order to have them ready for delivery, and to Beverly Jarrett for undertaking once again the editorial task of cleaning up my punctuation and prose.

THE PERSISTENT TRADITION
IN NEW SOUTH POLITICS

1 BOURBONS

THERE IS a kind of memorial impulse that seizes historians, a way of discovering things when they are at the point of departure. The most conspicuous example probably is that of Frederick Jackson Turner, who discovered the significance of the frontier just as the frontier vanished. A more recent case in point, and one closer home, has been C. Vann Woodward's inquest into the strange career of Jim Crow, with findings that have sharply challenged the conventional wisdom about southern history. The insights gained from such inquiries would seem to bear out the observation that things in passing reveal themselves.

Maybe, then, it is time for a valedictory to the Solid South. The Solid South is passing into history, assuming that it is not about to book a return engagement under new management. Even so, too much has changed for things ever to be quite the same again. Perhaps it is now possible to view the Solid South as a closed chapter, to see it reveal itself in passing. It seems apparent that the region has crossed a major watershed, not only in its politics but in its economics and society as well; it has entered a post-New South which does not yet have a name. Yet, as we play the historian's game of carving the past into periods, into eras and epochs, we should not forget the admonition of an English historian, Marcus Cunliffe, that American historians have an excessive propensity for discovering watersheds. Continuities in history are seldom, if ever, completely broken. Tradition has a stubborn way of asserting itself.

Certainly the terminology of southern politics shows endurance. Whatever may have happened to Thomas Alexander's "persistent Whigs" in the postbellum South, persistent Bourbons and persistent Populists still flourish, if we are to credit the present-day pundits. Even skeptical historians still find these epithets useful. Two books that appeared in close succession several years ago offer parallels which illustrate the point.

In *Bourbonism and Agrarian Protest: Louisiana Politics, 1877–1900*, William I. Hair proposed a refinement of common usage. Instead of the usual Bourbons and Populists, he set forth a threefold design in which he divided the ruling orders between predatory Bourbons and high-minded Patricians. A striking parallel to his design appeared in Numan V. Bartley's *The Rise of Massive Resistance: Race and Politics in the South During the 1950's.* In place of Bourbons, Patricians, and Populists, Bartley postulated neo-Bourbons, business conservatives, and neo-Populists.

Has the continuity been all that clear? Or does this curious juxtaposition owe something to the prevalence of triangular patterns in Western culture: the Holy Trinity of Father, Son, and Holy Ghost; the Hegelian trinity of thesis, antithesis, and synthesis; the human qualities of body, mind, and soul? Even the Fleming lectures, like all Gaul, are divided into three parts. And I have chosen to explicate Bourbons, Populists, and Progressives as the orthodox trinity of New South politics.

According to C. Vann Woodward, the first of these three groups, whom he called Redeemers, "laid the lasting foundations in matters of race, politics, economics, and law for the modern South." One need not quarrel with that judgment to suggest, however, that the Populists and Progressives added significant elements to the foundations on which the structure of southern politics rose in the first half of the twentieth century. These catagories, of course, afford certain hazards, not least of which is the danger of what Winston Churchill called "terminological inexactitude." Another problem is the exclusion of certain groups, most conspicuously Negroes and Republicans, who, however, at best only approached the fringes of political power.

But the Bourbons, Populists, and Progressives afford complexity enough. Let us begin with the Bourbons. Even the derivation and definition of the word are elusive, not to mention the very pronunciation which assumed variations in the process of migration from France: Burrbon and Boorbon. In a sprightly essay entitled "The Urbane Bourbon," John K. Bettersworth called it one of "the most indefinable words ever used to describe Southern persons, places, and things, either solid or liquid." In either form it has a distinctively southern flavor—even though Grover Cleveland of New York and other Yankees were sometimes tagged as Bourbons, and a group of "Midwestern Bourbons" was stigmatized by Horace Samuel Merrill as "a cabal of industrialist-financier entrepreneurs operating within the Democratic party . . . to occupy the only really vulnerable outpost in the political-economic empire of big business" and "to sit on the lid of farmer and wage-earner opposition." The earliest American usage of the word, moreover, has been traced to the faraway territory of Washington where in 1859 the Olympia *Pioneer and Democrat* said: "The 'Bourbon' family have attempted to rule this territory from the earliest hour of its creation."

The exact date of its first application to the South remains unknown, but the term was in circulation well before 1873 when James S. Pike wrote in *The Prostrate State*: "It must be said of the Southern Bourbon of the Legislature that he comports himself with a dignity, a reserve, and a decorum, that command admiration." But admiration was scarcely signified by the common usage, which derived from Napoleon Bonaparte's pronouncement that the French royal family had forgotten nothing and learned nothing in the ordeal of the Revolution. Like the French Bourbons, it was said, the southern Bourbons had forgotten nothing and learned nothing in the ordeal of the Civil War. Through whatever channels, then, the name came to denote a mossback reactionary devoted to things past, to ideas that no longer fitted changed conditions, to the Old South, and to the Confederacy.

It functioned mainly as a pejorative epithet and few men could glory in the name. One of the rare exceptions was a Baton Rouge editor and mayor—a Bourbon with the unlikely name of Leon Jastremski—and even Jastremski would have preferred the title Stuart, in honor of the merry monarch Charles II and the English Restoration. It was not the post-Reconstruction leaders themselves, but their Republican, Independent, and Populist adversaries who applied the label so tenaciously that Bourbon came to signify the leaders of the conservative democracy—including not only the mossbacks but the advocates of an industrial New South, who, if they had forgotten nothing, had at least learned something. Like the other unfortunate epithets of the period—carpetbagger, scalawag, bloody shirt, outrage mills, bayonet rule, home rule (as a euphemism for white rule) —Bourbon became firmly embedded in the historical lexicon.

Not for want of effort to pry it out. C. Vann Woodward wrote in his biography of Tom Watson that "since the American aborigines were called *Indians* there has probably been no more fallacious misnomer in our history." Woodward proposed to substitute the term *New Departure Democrats*, with the realization, he wrote, "that all political epithets share the fault of slovenly thinking." He took his cue from the "New Departure" of 1872, which signified the Democrats' formal acquiescence to the Reconstruction amendments for the first time—in their national platform—and their endorsement of Horace Greeley on the Liberal Republican ticket. For Georgia at that time it could also have meant acceptance of former Governor Joseph E. Brown's advice to combine the "practical view of the businessman" with the duties of the "statesman" and to reject the views of unreconstructed rebels like Robert Toombs.

For the purpose intended, *New Departure Democrats* served better than the term *Redeemers*, which Woodward adopted in *Origins of the New South*. *Redeemers* has gained more widespread acceptance and usage, but with its freight of connotations about the evils of Reconstruction and the virtues of Redemption, the word carries about as much potential mischief as the term Bourbon itself.

But the problem of nomenclature is only a pale reflection of the more substantive problem of interpretation. "Class, race, and party have so complicated the contest for political power in the New South," Rupert Vance once wrote, "that historians have more difficulties with the period from redemption to 'democracy' than the revisionists and orthodox factions have with Reconstruction." As a matter of fact, interpretations of the two periods have been linked in an inverse relationship. So long as the Radicals of Reconstruction were low on the scales of historical judgment, the Bourbons stayed high. When the Radicals' stock began to rise the Bourbons' repute began to sink. All too often, either way, historians were caught up in what Bernard Weisberger called an "operatic version of history," replete with heroes and villains. Historians just disagreed on which was which.

Part of the trouble with the years after Reconstruction has been the apparent lack of dramatic appeal. The "most honorable period" in the history of the South, according to Philip A. Bruce, the Bourbon era lacked the color of romance and conflict which have drawn historians to the antebellum and Confederate South, to Reconstruction, to the Populist revolt. As Jacob E. Cooke put it: "The South after 1877, its position of preeminence in the councils of the nation gone and its economy and social order evidently conforming ever more closely to the national pattern, seemed to many an unrewarding study."

Further problems arise from the diversity of the studies which do exist. Unlike the Reconstruction monographs of the Dunning school, as Rupert Vance noted, the studies of Redemption have not been built to uniform specifications. Some treatments of the period emphasize economics, at least one takes the New South creed as a problem of intellectual history, others focus on race relations, and some pursue a biographical approach. Several state studies have appeared in the last two decades, but some of these cover a broader scope of political history than the Bourbon period alone. Consequently, as Jacob Cooke explained, the period "does not readily lend itself to historiographical discussion" because "few historians have presented a monistic interpretation which gives unity and meaning to the varied facts of Southern experience."

In the beginning, however, historians of the New South had no trouble with complexity. They wrote under the euphoric spell of Redemption and against a backdrop of alleged Reconstruction horrors and scandals that had threatened the very fabric of society. To their minds the Bourbon regimes exemplified the triumph of honor and justice. Every state supplied its quota of pietistic paeans to the leaders of Redemption. The chief function of these leaders, Philip A. Bruce explained in the first general history of the period, his *The Rise of the New South* (1905), had been to cut away the "poisonous growth" of Reconstruction and restore a climate of political order in which economic growth could flourish. The real story, ultimately, was the new birth of prosperity, and to that Bruce devoted most of his book. For years, as David Potter has noted, the historiography of the period remained in a primitive condition, riddled with clichés about Redemption, the New South, the elimination of the corrupt Negro vote, and the like. Holland Thompson, the first academic historian to survey the period, in *The New South* (1919), acknowledged the existence of political opposition, questioned the Bourbon's penny-pinching, and deplored the unproductive role of Confederate brigadiers in Congress; but even he wrote that no "governments in American history have been conducted with more economy and more fidelity than the governments of the Southern States during the first years after the Reconstruction period."

Revisionism had scarcely appeared before the 1930s, and when it came it slipped in by the back door, so to speak, in studies of populism for which the Bourbon era was an indispensable background. Historians of populism, by focusing on the Bourbons' opponents, moved the critique of Bourbonism front and center. And because they did not boggle at derogatory connotations, they fixed among historians the populistic habit of using Bourbon as a generic term for the post-Reconstruction establishment. The Bourbons have had a bad press ever since.

Alex M. Arnett began the process as early as 1922, in *The Populist Movement in Georgia.* A new image of Bourbonism began to emerge in the 1930s, mainly in the growing literature on populism, and finally sprang full-blown from the pages of C. Vann Woodward's *Reunion and Reaction* and his *Origins of the New South,* both published in 1951. Instead of unity, Woodward found in the Bourbon South evidence of sharp political divisions that involved race, class, party, and intrastate sectionalism. "The classic lines of cleavage in Southern society were not erased magically by Reconstruction," he wrote.

Instead of absolute fidelity Woodward found corruption and peculation, the arch-thief being Louisiana's state treasurer, E. A. Burke, who left the accounts a million dollars short when he embarked for Tegucigalpa. Instead of disfranchising Negro voters completely, Woodward noted, the Redeemers of the Black Belt controlled (or at least counted) a captive Negro vote to save the "party of white supremacy" from hillbilly insurgents. Bourbon state governments made a cardinal virtue of retrenchment and cut back sharply on expenditures for schools and other public services. Finally, and most importantly, they absorbed most of the old Whigs and took on a Whiggish coloration. They may have worshipped at the shrine of the old order, but they embraced a new order of economic development. They perfected a political alliance with eastern conservatives and an economic alliance with the robber barons. They invited a new generation of financial carpetbaggers to colonize the South and exploit its resources, including its cheap labor, and they enriched themselves through convict-leasing, corporate retainers, and other benefits of favoritism.

The pattern has become so familiar that it is hard to remember how completely Woodward's revisionism gutted the old baroque structure of southern historiography. At the time of writing, Woodward had few monographs available on which to base his new design, and none of these was in print except the early studies of populism. The one that most completely supported his interpretation was Judson C. Ward's unpublished dissertation on Georgia's Bourbons. The new picture of the "business Bourbons," therefore, owed much to the study of Georgia, home of the most celebrated advocate of the New South, Henry W. Grady, and domain of the Bourbon triumvirate —Joseph E. Brown, John Brown Gordon, and Alfred H. Colquitt—all of whom had figured significantly in Arnett's study of populism and Woodward's biography of Tom Watson. In the year that *Origins of the New South* was published, two more state monographs appeared: Allen Going's *Bourbon Democracy in Alabama* and A. D. Kirwan's *Revolt of the Rednecks: Mississippi Politics, 1876–1925*, both of which substantially supported Woodward's analysis but indicated a somewhat greater strength of agrarian elements in those states than in Georgia.

Subsequent studies have confirmed the new orthodoxy more often than they have challenged it—with one exception. William J. Cooper's *The Conservative Regime: South Carolina, 1877–1900*, took a drastic departure from the image of "business Bourbons." It is an almost unparalleled picture of the classic Bourbons in the original sense of those who clung obstinately to the past:

> The theme of the Confederacy and of times past pervaded the Conservative mind. The South Carolina Conservatives looked forward not to a better world but to a re-created one. For them, the best of all possible worlds had existed in antebellum South Carolina. To build anew what they revered in that commonwealth became their cardinal purpose. . . . The tangible and real problems of industrialization and agricultural depression failed to challenge men thinking in the past tense.

The growing literature on the Bourbons still does not approach in weight or scope the outpouring of publications on the Confederacy and Reconstruction, and it leaves an element of unresolved paradox in its appraisal of the Bourbon leadership. For instance, how are we to assess the significance of men like James Z. George, who is usually assigned a place in Mississippi's Bourbon triumvirate? According to a study by May Spencer Ringold, George remained a friend of the poor class from which he had risen. He "consistently urged the extension of governmental functions to encompass a control of big business and the regulation of railroads; his tariff policy was hostile to the industrial East; and on the question of bankruptcy and financial legislation, he fostered the interests of the debtor, the consumer, and the small businessman." What are we to make of the fact that Bourbon regimes, which presumably upheld the sanctity of property, repudiated state debts in wholesale lots, while a Conservative regime in Virginia defended the obligation of debt so insistently and at such cost that it was temporarily overthrown by an Independent rebellion, the Readjuster Movement? How do we deal with the Bourbons' approach to race relations, since these paragons of white supremacy tolerated a lingering Negro voice in politics and showed no haste about raising the barriers of racial separation? How do we resolve the paradox that these niggardly regimes, so ardently devoted to laissez faire, established railroad commissions to regulate rates, boards of agriculture, boards of public health, agricultural experiment stations, agricultural and mechanical colleges, normal schools, and women's colleges, even state colleges for Negroes?

Perhaps we begin to comprehend the problem by recognizing that the Democratic party of that period was, to use Allen Moger's phrase, a "mongrel coalition" which threw old Whigs, Know-Nothings, unionists, secessionists, businessmen, small farmers, hillbillies, planters, even some Republicans together in alliance against the Reconstruction Radicals. Once Redemption was achieved, the conflicts inherent in any coalition began to assert themselves so that Bourbon regimes never achieved monolithic unity either in philosophy or government.

Tennessee perhaps best illustrates the point, for factionalism in the Democratic party there reached perhaps its clearest definition and most even balance of forces. There, according to Dan M. Robison's *Bob Taylor and the Agrarian Revolt in Tennessee,* the old-line Whigs and new-line businessmen gave rise to what was called the Whig-industrialist wing, a group infused with the ideas of Henry Clay and led by Arthur S. Colyar. Two more factions carried over from the prewar Democrats: a states' rights-secessionist-planter group infused with the ideas of Calhoun and led by Isham G. Harris, and a farmer-workingman group infused with the ideas of Jacksonian Democracy and led by Andrew Johnson.

After Johnson's death in 1875, however, his following in the rural democracy lapsed into relative apathy for more than a decade. Meanwhile, conflict between the Whig-industrialists and Harris wings over issues of debt repudiation and railroad regulation divided the party so badly that the Republicans elected a governor in 1880, and ran close races in 1882 and 1884. The Democratic party was finally revitalized in 1886 by the rise of Robert Taylor, an earthy raconteur and fiddle-playing East Tennessean who became Andrew Johnson's belated successor and revived the enthusiasm of the rural Democrats. Bob

Taylor was uniquely qualified to play the role of unifier. Offspring of a Whig-unionist father who went Republican after the war, adversary of a Republican brother who ran against him for governor in the so-called War of the Roses, Taylor took his own political cue from a Democratic uncle. His family included both unionists and Confederates, and his policy of prudent moderation in affairs of state prevented serious affront to either the Whig or the Harris wing. When populism appeared in the 1890s Bob Taylor emerged once again and almost literally laughed the Tennessee farmers out of it.

Not every state had a Bob Taylor. Even in Tennessee agrarian mavericks kept wandering off the reservation, and the history of the Bourbon era abounds in examples of rebellious Independents, sometimes in uneasy alliance with blacks and Republicans. These Independents endorsed a variety of heterodox proposals: debt repudiation, inflation, usury laws, antimonopoly laws. Locally they fought Bourbon Democrats over fencing laws, the dominance of courthouse rings, and a variety of personal complaints. Philip A. Bruce clearly ignored the evidence and begged the point when he wrote: "War and Reconstruction served only to strengthen the homogeneity of the people of the Southern States . . . by welding the native whites into the most perfect oneness for the preservation of all they cherished." Any Virginian who lived through the Readjuster Movement, as Bruce did, should have known better than that. Yet there was a germ of truth in his claim. The cement of the Democratic coalition was its role as the savior and defender of southern civilization from the combined threats of external intervention and internal chaos. And white supremacy was the rallying-cry which summoned the white masses to the defense of the community.

According to the nostalgic romances which swept the region and the whole nation during the 1880s, the southern civilization had reached its zenith on the old-time plantation. The life of the Old South, Thomas Nelson Page wrote, was "the purest, noblest life ever lived." And it was lived, increasingly, through the haze of nostalgia, in a society that was stable, ordered, organic, and if not hierarchical, at least deferential. The planter element, Eugene Genovese has maintained, "commanded southern politics and set the tone of social life. Theirs was an aristocratic, anti-bourgeois spirit with values and mores emphasizing family and status, a strong code of honor, and aspirations to luxury, ease and accomplishment. In the planters' community, paternalism provided the standard of human relationships, and politics and statecraft were the duties and responsibilities of gentlemen." "Every community," John De Forest noted in postwar South Carolina, "has its great man, or its little man, around whom his fellow citizens gather when they want information, and to whose monologues they listen with a respect akin to humility." De Forest called him the "central monkey."

Habits of deference, moreover, pervaded the society and outlived the planter regime. "A value definition of a society," William D. Miller has argued, "having been established as 'true,' is customarily accepted by all classes of that society as long as the mythic form that gives rise to these values maintains stability." What is more, he adds, "As the root sources of the life of a mythic structure ebb, especially in the pain of defeat, the impulse to community becomes strident."

On the whole, James G. Randall once said, poets and novelists have been better at evoking the oneness of community than historians have been at explaining it. Nearly every major work of the southern literary renaissance of the twentieth century has been built around the conflict between southern tradition and modernity. But, unlike twentieth-century writers who had in a sense "outgrown the dimensions" of community and who looked back from new perspectives acquired in travel and education, nineteenth-century southern authors were too deeply immersed in the community, too involved in its life and traditions, to see it in a critical perspective. Instead, with notable exceptions like Mark Twain and George W. Cable, they celebrated a land where, in the words of historian Paul H. Buck:

Men and women had lived noble lives and had made noble

sacrifices to great ideas, where Negroes loved "de white folks," where magnolias and roses blossomed over hospitable homes that sheltered lovely maids and brave cadets, where the romance of the past still lived . . . a Dixie of the storybooks which had become the Arcady of American tradition.

Few men expressed with more clarity the force of this tradition and the intense emotions it aroused than one writer who stood outside the tradition and viewed it with a jaundiced eye. Fourteen years a carpetbagger in North Carolina, Albion W. Tourgée later exploited his experience in two novels of Reconstruction, *A Fool's Errand* (1880) and *Bricks Without Straw* (1881).

The southern white, he wrote in the latter, viewed "the downfall of the Confederacy as the triumph of a lower and baser civilization—the ascendancy of a false idea and an act of unrighteous and unjustifiable subversion." Enfranchisement of the blacks was only the crowning infamy. "Perhaps," Tourgée wrote, "there is not a single Northern resident of the South who has not more than once offended some personal friend by smiling in his face while he raged with white lips and glaring eyes, about this culminating ignominy. . . . Regarding it as inherently fraudulent, malicious, and violent, he felt no compunctions in defeating its operation by counterfraud and violence. . . .

"Of course, in this counter-revolution there was not any idea of propagating or confirming the power of the political party instituting it! It was done simply to protect the State against incompetent officials. The people were not wise enough to govern themselves, and could only become so by being wisely and beneficently governed by others, as in the ante-bellum era. From it, however, by a *curious accident*, resulted that complete control of the ballot and the ballot-box by a dominant minority so frequently observed in those states.

"It was all without question," Tourgée finished sarcastically, "the result of wise and patriotic legislation."

As Tourgée saw so clearly, the defense of the community had a way of becoming the defense of vested interest and class distinctions, and vice versa. Such a connection was at work earlier in the secession movement, as it would be later in responses to populism and the New Deal. The election of Abraham Lincoln, Roy Nichols suggested in *The Disruption of American Democracy*, raised less fear of what the new president might accomplish in direct antislavery action than of what he might do with his control of the patronage. "He would be appointing a postmaster in every community. Where would he find the men? Not among the aristocracy, not among the fire-eaters, not among the Democrats. Might they not be men of his own humble origin? . . . They would preach to the poor against the rule of the rich and would stir up a class struggle to create a new order in the name of democracy." However inflated the fears, it was plausible that Lincoln could work to undermine deference to the planting class, the loyalty of southern whites and the submission of southern slaves to the existing community.

Reconstruction brought such things to pass, and worse. It threatened civilization itself with the very anarchy that had overwhelmed Santo Domingo years before. The future mythology of Reconstruction already was taking shape before the Radicals secured their grip, in for example the Charleston *Mercury*'s fulminations against "the ringed, striped, and streaked" convention of 1868 which it confidently foretold would bring anarchy and confiscation upon the state. In the future such judgments would become a staple of Democratic propaganda, best summarized in a volume entitled *Why the Solid South?* which a group of southern congressmen assembled in 1890 as an argument against the Lodge elections bill, which they called the "force bill." State by state they reviewed Reconstruction in terms that would shape the image of its history for more than fifty years. Eventually the Democratic mythology of Reconstruction became the staple of historiography as well as public discourse.

That in itself was no mean achievement, but the ultimate achievement of the Bourbons was that of all durable conservative movements: the reconciliation of tradition with innovation. Their relative moderation in racial policy was one manifestation of an ability to accommodate just enough of the new to disarm their adversaries and perhaps a clue that class interest was more important to them than racial dogma. By accepting another new truth, the Industrial Revolution, the Bourbons led the South into a new order, but without sacrificing what Francis B. Simkins called "the pageantry and rhetoric of the sentimental South." The Bourbons did this, Simkins wrote, "by a matchless display of diplomacy worthy of a Talleyrand. They not only won for themselves a subordinate but dignified place in the councils of the nation but also for their people a share in the national prosperity." And they were "deft enough to win at the hands of the victorious North, honors for the Confederacy after it was dead."

In the transition they produced no master ideologue, no John Locke or Edmund Burke. They had as their vindicators instead those prophets of a New South like Francis W. Dawson and Henry W. Grady who asserted that the fatal defect of the Old South was the lack of a balanced economy. These men envisioned a South which venerated its past, but sought a progressive future of industrial development and agricultural diversification. To create the needed climate of stability they preached reconciliation: North and South, Old South and New, farmer and businessman, rich and poor, white and black. In the process they created the New South creed, a mythology as potent as the myths of the plantation, the Confederacy, and Reconstruction, all of which they incorporated to buttress the new order. "By the twentieth century, then," Paul

The Persistent Tradition in New South Politics

Gaston has written, "there was established for many in the South a pattern of belief in which they could see themselves and their section as rich, success-oriented, and just. . . . Just as the fair picture of the ante-bellum South gave Southerners courage and pride while at the same time offering blandishments to Northern antagonism, so the picture of a New South had the double effect of ameliorating the bleak realities of the present and winning approbation from the world outside."

While inventing a New South, the Bourbons kept alive the vision of an organic traditional community with its personal relationships, its class distinctions, its habits of deference to the squirearchy. And it was more than a romantic image tucked away in some corner of the mind, to be summoned up in moments of euphoria. The sense of community remained a living tradition of the people, buttressed by the romantic myth but also a living reality. The Bourbons assimilated industry into their patterns of rustic virtue. The paternalism (and rapacity) of the planters entered the board rooms, and the folkways of the yeomen entered the factory. The leaders of the New South pursued, in a peculiarly southern way, that quest for reconciliation between old verities and new truths in society which on the larger American scene Robert Wiebe has called *The Search for Order*. In the 1890s their search would be rudely interrupted by the Populists, who sought another road to salvation, but after 1900 it would be renewed by the Progressives, the successors and heirs of the Bourbons, who preserved tradition under the rubric of reform.

II POPULISTS

During the 1972 campaign, the casual reader must have had the impression that the country harbored more Populists per square mile than at any time since 1896. In the capricious world of political high fashion, the "new populism" was for a season all the go, the biggest thing since radical chic. Now the pundits are off to pastures new and the historians can get back to the real thing. But it will not be easy. We can hardly avoid confusion when we remember that the rubric *populism* covered everybody from Spiro Agnew to Bella Abzug or from George Wallace to George McGovern. And what is one to make of that "band of populist sinners and dancers" that, according to *Time*, gyrated through Leonard Bernstein's *Mass*? Or those "populist portfolio managers" to whom, according to *Newsweek*, investors were turning? We may well doubt that many real Populists were ever found in the concert hall or on Wall Street. The party of course did harbor a few termagants who might pep up the fem lib movements today, but even they would no doubt be mystified by *Ms.* magazine and its monthly column of homely advice on "Populist Mechanics."

The "new populism" was not the first wave of fashion to leave behind an overlay of confusion. The variant definitions now exceed those attached to *Bourbon* or, for that matter, any but a few other political epithets. Complication set in early. The word *Populist*, invented in Kansas some eighty-odd years ago as a name for supporters of the People's party, became within a few years the standard translation for the Russian *narodnik*, who represented something quite different, despite superficial parallels. The translation was a semantic accident, though a logical analogy—both words have roots meaning "people"—but the usage has been a source of infinite distraction. In more recent years, chiefly in the last two decades, populism has acquired still other variations.

For some writers populism means a celebration of the *Volksgeist*, the spirit of the folk. For others it may indicate theories of the popular will and suggest the tyranny of the majority or the spirit of popular conformity which so impressed de Tocqueville in nineteenth-century America. Social scientists have come to use *populism* indiscriminately as a label for popular movements, especially in the "Third World." Recently it has emerged and apparently subsided as the rallying-cry for a political movement—the new populism. And finally, it has become a vogue word among journalists for any person or thing which appeals to the masses of the common folk. For some writers populism seems to have acquired the status of an actual on-going phenomenon in our society, waiting only to be recognized or at most to be mobilized.

In order to retrieve the prototype of the 1890s, we must first peel off the layers of variant meaning which have built up over the years. It used to be that anybody with an elementary grasp of American history knew that a Populist was an adherent of the People's party, which flourished in the 1890s. The movement sprang chiefly from the rural South and West and derived from deep-seated grievances caused by the decay of the farmer's economic condition. It climaxed two decades of agitation by grangers, greenbackers, and Farmers' Alliancemen. Populism won few elections, but it fulfilled what has been the historical function of third parties in American politics. It gave voice to discontent. It advanced new issues and it forced the major parties to take them up.

The Populist platform of 1892 was almost a checklist of reforms to come. It called for currency inflation, farm credit, a graduated income tax, and postal savings banks. Other planks demanded government ownership of railroads and the reservation of public lands for actual settlers. Political and economic demands included the secret ballot, the initiative and the referendum, popular election of senators, a single term for president and vice-president, and, in a gesture toward urban workers, the eight-hour day and restriction of immigration. Condemnations of the tariff and of subsidies to corporations rounded out the platform. State platforms demanded improvements in education, tax reform to reduce the burden of levies on land, fertilizer inspection, usury laws, and the abolition of convict-leasing.

In 1892 presidential candidate James B. Weaver of Iowa polled twenty-two electoral votes and better than a million popular votes on the Populist ticket. A severe depression after the Panic of 1893 seemed to destine the Populists for major-party status, but in the next three years President Cleveland's effort to save the gold standard focused attention more and more on the currency. In 1896 William Jennings Bryan preempted the silver issue and ran off with both Democratic and Populist nominations. The Populists, amid recriminations over Bryan's refusal to accept their vice-presidential candidate, Tom Watson of Georgia, went down in the general defeat of Bryan.

Southerners, living in a more settled community with deeper traditions than the new states of the West, moved more reluctantly into the Populist rebellion than did westerners. The switch was akin to religious conversion and was often made at the cost of rejection by friends and family; but once the decision was taken, Populists in the South became all the more stubborn in their demands. During 1890, farmers who had been drawn into the Farmers' Alliance held aloof from the earliest third-party efforts which upset the political balance in the West, especially in Kansas. But they scored equal if not greater successes within the Democratic party by forcing the nomination of candidates pledged to their program: Governors W. J. Northen of Georgia, Benjamin R. Tillman of South Carolina, John P. Buchanan of Tennessee, James S. Hogg of Texas. Alliance candidates won majorities in seven legislatures, about forty seats in the national House of Representatives and several in the Senate (no exact count is possible since one cannot measure exactly the degree of a candidate's commitment to the farmers' program).

Success fostered agitation for a third party. Late in 1891 Georgia's Congressman Thomas E. Watson joined a caucus of Populists from the West and announced that his state was ready for the third party. But a major break did not come until it became apparent that the national Democratic party would nominate Grover Cleveland again. Southern Populists contested elections for the first time in 1892. In some places they perfected fusions with Republicans and in other places got Republican support or endorsement. In Alabama, which proved to be the banner Populist state in the South, Reuben F. Kolb, leader of the agrarian Democrats, claimed to have been robbed of the Democratic nomination for governor and ran on a "Jeffersonian Democratic" ticket that had the endorsement of Populists and Republicans. In the end he was counted out on the basis of an inflated vote from the Black Belt counties, which the Democrats controlled. The same thing would happen again in 1894, whereupon Kolb took the oath of office anyway but failed to make good his claim after he refused to countenance the use of force. But in several states—Florida, the Carolinas, Georgia, Texas—Democratic platforms borrowed Populist doctrines. In South Carolina the Tillmanite Farmers' Association so tightened its grip on the Democratic machinery that the third party never made headway. In Georgia the Populists lost out completely to wholesale manipulation by the Democrats. The major stumbling block was the issue of white supremacy, which the Democrats exploited with a seasoned finesse even while they controlled, or at least counted, the Negro vote in the Black Belts. Throughout the South, in 1892 and subsequently, the Populists fell victim to invective, intimidation, ballot-box stuffing, vote-buying, and physical violence.

This was the almost universal fate of the party in the region. Only in North Carolina did the Populists approach power at the state level, and even there they won the legislature in 1894 and 1896 only in a mismatched fusion with Republicans. By reducing the Democratic vote, moreover, they brought about the election of a Republican governor. In 1896, after the Democrats had nominated Bryan, southern Populists by and large provided the fiercest opposition to a strategy of coalition with the Democrats whom they had fought at such heavy cost. Forced to yield, they found themselves in a perplexing situation: collaborating with Democrats in the national election and with Republicans in state and local elections. This experience, on top of repeated frustrations, finally destroyed the movement. Such, in outline, are the short, if not so simple, annals of the People's party in the South.

After 1896 farm prices improved and the People's party faded away. The focus of the reform spirit in the nation shifted to the cities, where middle-class Progressives attacked problems of urban development, political bossism, and industrial monopoly. The precise role of populism as a forerunner to progressivism is still a subject of controversy, but during the years down to World War I an amalgam of rural and urban reformers produced a body of legislation that fulfilled much of the Populist program, and more besides. There was little question among former Populists, for the most part, and among some of their adversaries, that populism had received a certain vindication.

Such an interpretation eventually came to dominate the literature of southern populism. At the time, however, southern intellectuals, like their northern counterparts, avoided the movement and regarded it as a threat to stability. In their writings they tended to ignore it altogether. Bruce's *The Rise of the New South*, for instance, avoided the slightest mention of the movement, in fact virtually ignored politics. Southern populism did not begin to enter historiography until Holland Thompson in 1919 devoted a chapter of *The New South* to the farmers' revolt and Alex Arnett in 1922 published the first substantial monograph on the subject, *The Populist Movement in Georgia*. As late as 1932 Virginius Dabney could slight populism in his study of *Liberalism in the South* and William Watts Ball, in *The State That Forgot*, could write off the Tillman movement as a momentary aberration.

It was only as the decade of depression and New Deal advanced that populism reached its apotheosis. In 1931 John D. Hicks brought out his classic study, *The Populist Revolt*, in which the Populists emerged as a group clearly in the liberal tradition, the heirs of Jacksonian Democracy and the precursors of progressivism. Hicks focused on the movement mainly as a western phenomenon, but he established an orthodox doctrine that to the present day has pervaded the monographs on southern populism, beginning with Roscoe C. Martin's *The People's Party in Texas* (1933) and continuing in a host of studies, which are conveniently summarized in an essay

The Persistent Tradition in New South Politics

by Allen J. Going in Link and Patrick (eds.), *Writing Southern History* (1965). During the age of depression and New Deal, as Vann Woodward has observed, historians had little difficulty in developing an affinity for populism. The two periods had so much in common: a setting of depression, a feeling of desperation about farm problems and unemployment, antagonism toward big business, a sense of urgency about reform.

Throughout the twenty years of the New and Fair Deals the Populists remained in good odor among those intellectuals who embraced the neo-Populistic farmer-labor-liberal coalition of Franklin D. Roosevelt. Their euphoric approval of the Populist heritage prevailed into the 1950s. Then in 1955 historian Richard Hofstadter handed up a startling indictment. The Populists, he charged in *The Age of Reform: From Bryan to F. D. R.,* had sought scapegoats more than solutions, had suffered paranoid delusions of conspiracy by the "Money Power," had fostered antisemitism, xenophobia, jingoism, parochialism, and feverish visions of cataclysm. Populist thinking, Hofstadter suggested, "has survived in our own time, partly as an undercurrent of poular resentments, popular and 'democratic' rebelliousness and suspiciousness, and nativism."

Other writers, less careful than Hofstadter, and less steeped in history, located in populism the fountainhead of American fascism, the radical right, anti-intellectualism, McCarthyism, witch-hunting, and other malignities. Such writers, however, revealed more about the anxieties of urban intellectuals in the 1950s than about populism in the 1890s. Behind their treatment of populism the sinister figure of Joseph McCarthy lurked against a backdrop of loyalty oaths and witch-hunts. Intellectuals had rediscovered the seamy side of democracy, and by some kind of spontaneous combustion they hit upon *populism* as the modern equivalent for an outmoded word, *mobocracy*. According to the poet and publicist Peter Viereck, populistic attitudes "underlay Robespierre's Committee of Public Safety" and later "our neo-Populist Committee on un-American Activities."

Hofstadter had focused on the historic Populists and had carefully qualified his arguments. He admitted to rigging the scales in order to rectify the balance, but one can no longer evaluate populism without weighing certain components which earlier historians neglected. Yet one need not conclude that populism bore a unique burden of those evils, which pervaded American society, nor that it was a supreme force in disseminating them.

Insofar as the critics of populism were reading back into the 1890s the anxieties of the 1950s, their argument has been pretty much exploded by later studies. C. Vann Woodward's essay, "The Populist Heritage and the Intellectual" (1959), suggested most of the counterarguments and admonished intellectuals against repudiating the heritage of movements which "shock the seats of power and privilege and furnish the periodic therapy that seems necessary to the health of our democracy." Michael Rogin's *The Intellectuals and McCarthy* (1967) not only shattered the notion that Joseph McCarthy was heir to populism but advanced a telling critique of theorists who interpret "efforts by masses to improve their condition as threats to stability" and turn "all threats to stability into threats to constitutional democracy." In *The Populist Response to Industrial America* (1962), Norman Pollack may have gone too far, but in that book he made the Populists out as pretty sophisticated political theorists. The more recent studies of populism in the South have for the most part held to orthodox doctrine, moreover, and have scarcely acknowledged the metropolitan critics of the 1950s.

Still, like other waves of fashion, the critique of the 1950s has left its residue of interpretation. In the last two decades the word *populism* has acquired a dual quality. A Populist can be at the same time both Dr. Jekyll and Mr. Hyde. A few years ago three political scientists tackled the problem of definition with an article, "In Search of Populism." The article, by James Clotfelter, William Hamilton, and Peter Harkins, appeared in *New South*, a publication of the Southern Regional Council. Unlike some of our hurried journalists, the authors of this article acknowledge the "vagueness of the populist notion" which "stems partly from the inconsistencies of historical

American populism." Still, they seem persuaded that there is something out there called populism, waiting only to be discovered and mobilized. Their research, however, is grounded mostly in examples of hostility that turn up in polling-samples of white southerners.

For these authors Populist attitudes include support for social-welfare measures (unless they are linked to blacks or to taxes), endorsement of "populist-flavored 'alienation' or 'cynicism' statements" ("It's still hard for the average man to get a fair shake"), and making scapegoats of groups perceived as threatening (a mixed bag of subversives, deadbeats, liberals, intellectuals, big corporations, and, above all, blacks). Populism encompasses "groups below the median in social class or income, but not usually including the poor and the destitute"—in short "Middle America" and "The Silent Majority."

In this piece populism seemed to be little more than an assortment of ill-focused discontents and prejudices. Yet the tone of the article held out the hope that a renewed populism, like its ancestor, might redirect massive grievances away from neurotic resentment and toward rational goals. Two of the same authors, Clotfelter and Hamilton, pursued this theme further in an essay, "Beyond Race Politics: Electing Southern Populists in the 1970's," in which they speculated on the possibility of biracial coalitions in the future. Their view parallels that of the American Civil Liberties Union lawyer, Charles Morgan, Jr., who sees populism as a positive and enduring force in southern politics: "To me, a Populist means the kind of political candidate who appeals to a broad base of voters, the broadest base of the poor and the oppressed and the underprivileged, whether that's Negro or white."

Such views, and much of the historical writing, have given to the populism of the 1890s a faint afterglow of romance strangely like that which brightens the memory of an earlier and more celebrated Lost Cause. Populism may have failed, but it won vindication in its sequel and in some mysterious way it still lives in the traditions of the people. It is the liberals' Lost Cause.

Among the early historians of the New South, while others ignored the movement, there *was* one who assigned it a major significance. In 1908 William Garrott Brown pronounced an oft-quoted judgment on the farmers' movement: "I call that particular change a revolution, and would use a stronger term if there were one; for no other political movement—not that of 1776, nor that of 1860–1861—ever altered Southern life so profoundly." The judgment, if excessive, carries an ironic kernel of truth. Like the movement of 1860–1861, the People's party failed. Yet if one set out to show positive consequences that flowed from the movement, as most of its historians have done, it is possible to establish a degree of vindication in the twentieth century. The Populist view that government should play a more positive role in righting wrongs, in dealing with the evils of society, did something to shatter encrusted theories that had prevented new governmental responsibilities and thereby paved the way for the Progressive movement. Surely the leaven of populism was at work in the southern education movement of the early twentieth century. In a sense the Democratic primary fulfilled Populist demands for greater democracy, albeit democracy for whites only. Progressive efforts for tax equalization followed Populist demands, at least at a distance. The Farmers' Union, founded in 1902, kept alive the Populist rhetoric and led a campaign for better warehousing which swept the region before the teens. The social justice movement owed something to the Populists' concern for the poor and rejected in society. What Woodward called the "Bryanization" of the Democratic party affected the South more strongly than any other region and persisted longer there than in Bryan's Nebraska. Many a southern Democrat, right on down to Huey Long and Lyndon Johnson, trailed clouds of glory from the heritage of populism. The process of Bryanization swept both major parties out of the ruts in which they had moved for a generation and brought them face to face with problems of reform in political institutions, currency, business regulation, and other fields—problems which the Populists had thrust upon them. On the national scene within a few decades most of their demands had been enacted into law.

Yet so much of all this remains in the realm of inference that we can still do little more than echo the judgment of William DuBose Sheldon, historian of Virginia populism, that "agitational background for democratic reform" was the principal achievement of the Populists. Almost without exception, the historians of populism have given more attention to the movement's origins in the farm discontent of the nineteenth century than to its lingering influence in the twentieth.

One recent study, however, focuses on the latter question: Sheldon Hackney's *Populism to Progressivism in Alabama* advanced a vigorous challenge to the view that the Populists were forerunners of the Progressives. Hackney's evidence led him to conclude that the rank and file of Alabama Populists, insofar as they remained politically active, drifted less back into the Democratic ranks than into the feeble Republican party, and that Progressives found less support among old Populists than among businessmen, professionals, and Black Belt planters. Some evidence of a similar development exists in the experience of Marion Butler, one-time senator and national chairman of the Populist party, who joined the Republicans and whose home county, Sampson, became a unique enclave of Republicanism in eastern North Carolina. How widely this was the sequence all across North Carolina and other states we cannot judge without more quantitative studies like Hackney's on Alabama.

On the other hand, it is possible to find pathetic figures like Reuben F. Kolb of Alabama, twice a Populist candidate for governor, who made his peace with the Democratic potentates and became a perennial candidate for office. Known as "old Run Forever," he finally won a term in 1910 as commissioner of agriculture, back where he had started in 1886. But it is difficult to find many Populist leaders who provided a link with Progressive reform, or, for that matter, wielded much political clout after the turn of the century.

It is easier to infer a genealogical connection between the Populists and the latter-day "demagogues." There seems little question that the agrarians opened the way by awakening the farmers politically and by weakening their attitudes of deference to their betters—an overturning most vividly seen in Ben Tillman's humiliation of the South Carolina aristocrats. Tillman and Watson are examples of the Populist (or at least crypto-Populist) as demagogue, but how much connection was there otherwise? There is evidence that James K. Vardaman, Mississippi's white chief, carried a large vote of former Populists and that Theodore G. "The Man" Bilbo at least won the support of Frank Burkitt, one-time Populist candidate for governor. But Populists did not invent demagoguery, and they did not invent the grinding resentments of the masses in the South, and perhaps, thus, they do not deserve to shoulder the whole burden of responsibility.

Unlike the demagogues, who often did little more than offend propriety on the way to public office and then settle into complacent acquiescence, populism threatened to upset the very structure of the Bourbon order. The Populists drew their support mainly from those who subsisted on the fringes of the traditional community, little touched by its controlling myths. Hackney gives a summary description of their following in Alabama, based on both statistical and verbal evidence:

> Populists were only tenuously connected to society by economic function, by personal relationships, by stable community membership, by political participation, or by psychological identification with the South's distinctive myths. Recruited heavily from among the downwardly mobile and geographically transient, they were vulnerable to feelings of powerlessness. They were largely superfluous farmers or ineffectively organized workers who were not linked to influential Alabamians by kinship or close association. They tended to come from isolated areas, from areas experiencing extraordinary influxes of population, and from areas with increasingly large concentrations of tenant farmers. In any case, their opportunity for the sort of psychological integration with the state's social system that developed from long-term personal interaction was limited. Populists also tended to come from the ranks and regions of Alabama life where the Old South, the Lost Cause, and the New South were myths with very little resonance. Given their position in the social structure, it would have been pathological for them to insist on

conformity to the existing order. Those Alabamians who emphasized loyalty to the Democratic Party were expressing the need felt by well-organized sectors of the community for social solidarity and stability in a time of crisis. Populists were men who chose to resist the disorganizing forces in their lives by joining a protest movement.

Like the Bourbons, the Populists had no major philosopher, no Thomas Jefferson or Karl Marx, no grand ideology to explain their grievances and sustain their protest. Instead, Hackney contends, "all they had were conspiracy theories."

But they had something more systematic than that. There is evidence scattered in Populist journals, speeches, and letters that they developed a truly radical if amorphous critique of the existing society, which in some ways paralleled that of the Marxists. In what some historians have labeled "the producer rhetoric," Populists propounded, or rather assumed, a kind of labor theory of value—derived not from Marx, however, but from the same work ethic that warms the heart of Richard Nixon. The fundamental problem of society, they argued, was simply that the producing classes were wrongly denied the opportunity to enjoy the fruits of their labor, that they were too often underfed and poorly clad and ill-housed while plutocrats led a sybaritic existence founded on human misery. The existing society, therefore, embodied a fundamental antagonism between producers and parasites, workers and manipulators, "Dives and Lazarus," "the robbers and the robbed." In this antagonism farmers, urban workers, and small businessmen fell on one side; industrialists, bankers, and oligarchs on the other. The New Orleans *Issue,* one of the more radical agrarian journals, suggested that the workers of Louisiana were not as intelligent as bees, because the bees had sense enough to kill the parasitic drones in the hives.

The Populists' world view was sharply at variance with the vision of traditional community governed by its natural leaders, where each person found his place and where no real conflict of interest could exist. On the other hand, the "producer rhetoric" itself too glibly assumed a natural harmony of interests among the producing classes and too confidently foresaw a political alliance among them. Populism did draw a quantum of support from urban workers, but less in the East, where the numbers were greater, than in the South and West. In the South, moreover, the producer rhetoric provided the rationale for a political unity that rose above race. "You are kept apart that you may be separately fleeced of your earnings," Tom Watson said to the white and black tenants. "You are made to hate each other because upon that hatred is rested the keystone of the arch of financial despotism which enslaves you both. You are deceived and blinded that you may not see how this race antagonism perpetuates a monetary system which beggars both."

In Georgia, Watson openly appealed for black votes, appeared on the stump with black speakers, and once summoned militant whites to protect a black Populist who had been threatened with violence. There is plentiful evidence of biracial coalition all across the South. In 1892, for instance, Arkansas Populists wrote into their platform a resolution introduced by a Negro delegate that their object was "to elevate the downtrodden irrespective of race or color." Blacks often appeared as delegates to party conventions and members of party committees. In Texas the party sponsored an active campaign of speaking and organizing by a black leader, John B. Rayner. In North Carolina, by fusion with Republicans or by splitting the white vote, Populists contributed to the election of a few Negro Republicans as legislators and minor officeholders and one as congressman. When the Democrats rallied to the defense of white supremacy, however, white Populists faltered under pressure. In 1898 a campaign of threats and intimidation ended fusion control of the Tar Heel legislature. In other states, too, when the division of the white votes brought the Negro vote into new prominence, sometimes as the balance of power, the Democrats revived the issue of white supremacy, which had remained dormant in the 1880s.

The extent or the depth of the fleeting interracial unity inspired by populism, however, may easily be exaggerated. It represented expediency more than conviction, the search for votes wherever they could be found. Nor was it unique to Populists. Republicans and Democrats also sought black votes. Possibly with time, the Populist movement might have breached the color line significantly; but it hardly lasted long enough, and it was followed by a reaction that entrenched race antagonism all the more.

While it lasted, populism, like radicalism a generation before and the New Deal a generation after, menaced the power structure of the southern community. However moderate its specific demands may seem in the light of passing years, it posited a different world view and different system of politics. It sought to organize a party of radical reform based on a coalition of the lower orders, white and black, in conflict with the established powers of the community. However much the fear of an overturn may have been fueled by feverish illusions and the apocalyptic rhetoric of the times, that fear goes far to account for the ferocity of the response.

From the beginning of the 1890s the omens of catastrophe haunted leaders of the southern élite. Late in 1890 David Schenck of North Carolina confided to his diary that he "should not be surprised" if a "bloody Revolution" soon occurred. Several months earlier the secretary of the North Carolina Farmers' Alliance confided to Senator Zeb Vance his trepidation at the temper of his own following: "The people are very restless. We are on the verge of a revolution. God grant that it may be blood-less. It would be dangerous for me to talk to the people as I am talking to you. I never dare to say one word that will add to class feeling." Populist leaders and editors did little to allay the fears when they themselves resorted to talk of revolution.

The response of the Democratic party to the Populist challenge went beyond ordinary partisanship. The specter of Populists in alliance with Republicans and Negroes revived bitter memories of Reconstruction along with fantasies of communism and anarchy. "It will give you some idea of this bitterness," Milford W. Howard, a Populist congressman from Alabama, wrote later in his autobiography, "when I state that my own father would not hear me speak and said he would rather make my coffin with his own hands and bury me than to have me desert the Democratic party. This has been more than thirty years ago but some of the old feeling still slumbers and I have never been and never will be forgiven for my fall from grace." It may have been exaggeration, but it was not just metaphor when Henry Demarest Lloyd wrote in 1896: "The line between the old Democracy and Populism in the South is largely a line of bloody graves." Or when a southern Populist told Lloyd: "The feeling of the Democracy against us is one of murderous hate. I have been shot at many times. Grand juries will not indict our assailants. Courts will give us no protection." Years later an old-line Georgia Democrat was still defending the perpetration of fraud and violence. "We had to do it," he told Alex Arnett. "Those d____ Populists would have ruined the country."

To secure orderly civilization and the gentlemanly code of good government, the only effective response in the long run would be to disfranchise those who threatened them. It was imperative, Governor Murphy J. Foster told the Louisiana legislature in 1894, that "the mass of ignorance, vice and venality without any proprietary interest in the State" be disfranchised. In 1896, when the fusion movement, according to the Baton Rouge *Advocate*, posed "a grave menace to our civilization," Louisiana Democrats rescued civilization by stealing the election and proceeded within two years to complete their disfranchisement of "the mass of ignorance, vice and venality"—elements which, it is well known, have been absent from Louisiana politics ever since.

Few historians, I suspect, can review the history of southern populism without developing a sense of inevitability, a feeling that no other outcome was possible, given the force of tradition in a rural community and the weakness of the rebels, whose base was the inarticulate and ill-educated rustics. One may speculate that even a few victories by the People's party and its survival as an organized movement would have made a difference in the political and social structure of the region, in its world view and its organizing myths. The course of disfranchisement might have been altered or even blocked. In a continuing party competition the options might have been other than what they became. The outcome, however, constitutes one of those perennial ironies of history that pursue the best laid schemes—that the consequences of one's actions may be different from one's intentions.

For populism raised the apprehensions of the southern gentry, who intensified their appeal to the sense of traditional community, mobilized their forces, tightened their control of elections, modified their position, accepted a modicum of the new demands (most conspicuously free silver), and rode out the storm. If it must be said that the leaven of populism "Bryanized" the Democratic party, it must be said, too, that the leaven of tradition neutralized the People's party. Tradition had to make compromises, as it had done before; but strengthened by compromise, it survived. The collapse of populism brought in its train disfranchisement and the triumph of the Solid South, free at last from the threat of rebellion.

III PROGRESSIVES

IT USED to be that the definition of progressivism was about as simple as the definition of populism, if not more so. If you had a nodding acquaintance with American history, you knew that the Progressive movement of the early twentieth century was a democratic reform movement directed against the abuses of Gilded Age bosses and robber barons. According to Kansas editor William Allen White, progressivism was simply populism that had "shaved its whiskers, washed its shirt, put on a derby, and moved up into the middle class." Its goals were greater democracy, good government, the regulation of business, and social justice. The view of progressivism as democratic reform, pure and simple, harmonized with the self-image of Progressives themselves and permeated the earliest national histories of the movement.

This became the accepted reading of progressivism in

the South as well, beginning with Arthur S. Link's groundbreaking article, "The Progressive Movement in the South, 1870–1914," which appeared in 1946 and which grew out of Link's studies of the Wilson movement in the South. Link set out to challenge a common view that reform had never reached the benighted South. On the contrary, Link argued, the South had experienced "a far-reaching progressive movement" which, like the movement in the nation, had sought to wrest control from "the political bosses and restore it to the people." The movement may not have sprung directly from populism, but it sprang largely from the rural discontent which had bred populism and it derived much of its program from the Populists.

According to Link, the forerunners of the Progressives had formed a kind of *tertium quid* in the nineteenth-century world of Bourbons and Populists:

Throughout the decades of agrarian revolt, class agitation, and conflict, there remained a great number of Democrats who were neither Bourbons nor Populists, but middle-of-the-road progressives. As a general rule, this group found its recruits in the middle class of the South among the more prosperous farmers, small business men, school teachers, editors and other professional groups. They looked askance at the defection of the Populists and the conservatism of the Bourbons. But to a great degree the aims of the Southern progressives—popular education, reforms looking toward greater popular control of state governments, and the abandonment by the state governments of laissez faire as a guide for economic and social action—were much the same as those of the Populists.

The Progressive movement had brought about the establishment or strengthening of railroad commissions, party primaries, corrupt-practices legislation, the popular election of senators, the commissioner and city-manager forms of municipal government, child-labor and educational reforms. It was deficient, however, in its attitudes toward tenancy and race. Yet if the region remained backward in these respects, Link wrote, "it may none the less be stated with emphasis that there were few sections of the country in which the masses of the people were more powerful than in the South."

The interpretation was further elaborated in Woodward's *Origins of the New South*—although with greater reservations about the limitations of progressivism for white only—and still further detailed in writings by A. D. Kirwan, John Wells Davidson, Anne Scott, Dewey Grantham, and others. In retrospect, certain liberal predilections seem to have guided these authors. All of them belonged to a generation that reached maturity as historians during or just after the onset of southern conservative reaction against the New Deal, and all of them had an urge to challenge the simplistic image of unrelieved conservatism in the Solid South. Like Walter Hines Page in earlier years, or the historians of populism, or

Virginius Dabney in his *Liberalism in the South,* they
betrayed an impulse to get up a liberal genealogy for the
South, to show that the alleged solidity of the South had
been highly exaggerated.

Their writings, which cast light into shadowed areas,
nevertheless suffered from a difficulty which all historians
encounter in one way or another. David Potter once suggested that "when an historian has a strong ideological
commitment, a tension may be set up between his devotion to the commitment and his devotion to realism for
its own sake." This tension may then lead the historian to
"an inner struggle in which his historical realism is pitted
against his liberal urge to find constructive meanings in
the past for the affairs of the present."

To make such a criticism, however, is to be wise after
the event, to speak from an entirely different frame of
reference, one which has been afforded by other historians' reconsideration of the period. Perhaps, in the present
state of historiography, the safest generalization is to say
that the question of the definition (or, for that matter,
even the existence) of progressivism is infinitely more
complicated than it was even a decade ago. One of the
historians mentioned above, Dewey Grantham, has testi-
fied to the complexity of the problem: "To speak of the
progressive movement is to speak of an age, for, like Jacksonian democracy, it was extraordinarily diffuse in its
origins, pervasive in its import, and seminal in its heri-

tage." Progressivism was a "reform movement with no set leadership, no single platform, no disciplined organization, and no planned means of action." According to Jack Temple Kirby, progressivism "should be included with other enduring historical tags, such as the Enlightenment and the Romantic Movement, which cannot withstand rigorous definition."

Newer interpretations have only begun to be tested in the southern setting, and some not at all. Stephen Potter —the guru of gamesmanship—once said that the rejoinder which will confound any argument is: "Yes, but not in the South." It is "an impossible comment to answer," he says. In most cases, one may well suspect the new interpretations need to be qualified in the light of regional peculiarities. For instance, while it is often noted that Progressive leaders, North and South, were apt to come from the educated middle class and brought the movement a tone of respectability which populism never had, Richard Hofstadter has argued that they often came from people of established wealth and culture who experienced "status anxiety" about their standing in a changing world. It may well be that some element of status anxiety governed southern reactions to the invasion of northern capital and the perceived threat that it would gobble up small businessmen. The Progressive leaders, however— with conspicuous exceptions like Richard I. Manning of South Carolina—came from elements of upward mobility rather than established family. Given the spirit of community that prevailed in the region, they seemed to have suffered little sense of alienation.

Some historians have stressed the role of intellectual leaders in creating a climate of reform. In the South a distinguished group of intellectual and educational leaders, working at the periphery of politics, played a unique role in nurturing the far-reaching campaigns for public education and public health. But they produced little that was more than remotely comparable to the muckraking elsewhere, which was exposing the bosses and robber barons. Southern intellectuals were touting the New South creed and praising southern captains of industry as deliverers. Among such leaders as Edwin A. Alderman, William Garrott Brown, Charles W. Dabney, William E. Dodd, Charles D. McIver, A. J. McKelway, Edgar Gardner Murphy, Walter Hines Page, Julia Tutweiler, and Booker T. Washington, there seems again to have been a comfortable sense of identification with the community, despite a certain amount of fretting at narrowmindedness and shoddy reaction and a degree of impatience with the continued exploitation of child labor. They all decried the spirit of radicalism.

Certain historians, notably Samuel P. Hays and Robert H. Wiebe, have cut directly across the old theme of popular crusades to stress the role of businessmen who were beginning to recognize the advantages of modernization

and who promoted reform along the lines of efficiency
and rationalization, which became significant trends in
progressivism. And Wiebe has pursued this theme beyond his study of businessmen to organize the entire
history of four decades after Reconstruction under the
rubric of *The Search for Order, 1877–1920*. Progressivism, in this context, becomes the climax of a groping
response to the disorganizing influence of what the soci-
ologists call structural differentiation in society—which
is to say, growing specialization— and to the tendency
of people to find identity less in the local community than
in the business or profession to which they were com-
mitted. Progressivism sought to counter this fragmentation and to restore order and stability. Ultimately, a new
middle class of urban professionals developed the values
of "continuity and regularity, functionality and ration-
ality, administration and management" to cope with
twentieth-century problems. The outcome, in short, was
the triumph of a bureaucratic mentality which guided a
"government of continuous involvement."

Wiebe's theme looks promising indeed as a key to the
meaning of progressivism in the South—with the guarded
qualification that, in this region at least, the bureaucratic
mentality remained more subject to the traditional mentality than elsewhere. This point is emphasized especially
by two recent historians of southern progressivism: Ray-
mond H. Pulley and Jack Temple Kirby. Pulley's very

title, *Old Virginia Restored*, states his theme of progressivism as a culmination of Redemption, a return to the "Virginia ideals of class and order." After the long post-bellum interregnum of class and racial conflict and political corruption in the Gilded Age, Virginia was once again governed with relative decorum and integrity, but "the development of democratic institutions and attention to the voice of the people in public affairs was denied." Pulley concluded: "Within the broader concept of the American dream of liberty and equality for all men, the price of Virginia's progressive peace was indeed high."

Kirby's title, *Darkness at the Dawning*, states his theme of paradox—that progressive reform should be so intimately associated with the disfranchisement and segregation of Negroes. Kirby's book is the only survey and the best synthesis of southern progressivism that we have. It reduces the complexities of the movement "by declaring it dichotomous," representing on the one hand the rural antitrust tradition and on the other hand "the urban-based, professional-minded, bureaucratizing and centralizing mode of thought." It was the latter theme, however, which gained the ascendancy. Even farm groups abandoned mass movements in favor of rationalization and "businesslike" procedures.

Historians of the New Left persuasion, most notably Gabriel Kolko, have argued that the Progressive movement paradoxically represented the triumph of business conservatism, "the victory of big business in achieving the rationalization of the economy that only the federal government could provide." Kolko argued that the regulation of business turned out actually to be regulation *by* businessmen who used it to stabilize the chaotic and uncertain conditions created by unrestrained competition.

If the spectrum of interpretation can cover so wide a span, all the way from a movement for popular control to a movement that brought the triumph of big business, perhaps what we have is another classic case of that perennial historical irony in which our ends bear no relation to our goals. Or perhaps we have a paradox so overwhelming as to cast into doubt the very concept of progressivism itself. And one historian, in fact, has composed an obituary for the Progressive movement. In an article in *American Quarterly*, Peter G. Filene has argued that in view of the varied groups, objectives, and results that have been gathered under the rubric of *progressivism*, the concept of progressivism as an organizing principle for the early twentieth century must be junked in favor of some other frame of reference.

For want of an alternative, however, we seem to be left with progressivism for the time being. If, as one writer on the subject suggested as early as 1912, progressivism was inchoate and spoke "with many voices," if to many men it meant many things, we must attempt first a summary of what they were. And we should remember that although we speak of a Progressive movement, actually we have reference to the spirit of an age rather than an organized movement—much as when we speak of Jacksonian Democracy. Among the salient tendencies of the Progressive spirit were the themes of democracy and honesty in government: reforms such as the party primary to bring government closer to the people and corrupt-practices acts to insure good government. Second, the gospel of efficiency: good government meant not only democracy and honesty but reorganization to eliminate waste and futility. Third, corporate regulation, governmental action against corporate abuses and the threat of monopoly. Fourth, social justice: a variety of reforms from private charities to legislation against child labor and liquor. Fifth and finally, the public service concept of government: the extension of governmental responsibilities into a wide range of direct services to the people— good roads, education, public health and welfare, rural credits, conservation, and others.

All of these had their advocates and scored their triumphs in the South during the years before the First World War, under such leaders as Robert Glenn in North Carolina, Hoke Smith in Georgia, Braxton Bragg Comer in Alabama, and Napoleon Bonaparte Broward in Florida. Unfortunately, however, historians until recently have tended to confine their attention to the prewar years on the hypothesis that after the war progressivism was submerged under a tide of revulsion against idealism and reform. On the contrary, it was transformed through emphasis upon certain of its tendencies and the distortion of others. If we pursue progressivism into the 1920s we begin to find a transition from a democratic and anticorporation progressivism to a movement for efficiency and expanding public services. These two themes of progressivism were highlighted and extended in the 1920s. The other three—democracy, corporate regulation, and social justice—were dimmed or partially eclipsed.

Several factors served paradoxically to make progressivism more pervasive and at the same time to temper its militancy. It fell out that Wilsonian progressivism was associated in nearly every one of its major measures with the names of one or more southerners, from the Underwood-Simmons Tariff to the Smith-Hughes Act for aid to education. Powerful forces wedded even reluctant southerners to the Wilsonian leadership: the need for a party record of achievement, the spirit of party regularity, the use of the patronage, the existence of Progressive factions in the southern states. The entire effect was to "Wilsonize" the party much as it had been "Bryanized" before, to make progressivism the fashion, but to dilute its reform urge by reliance upon a relatively conservative leadership in Congress.

Meanwhile, the impulse for reform turned into a drive

for moral righteousness and conformity, into crusades against Charles Darwin and John Barleycorn—both of whom, however, survived the encounter. The middle-class leaders who gave progressivism its predominant tone had fought largely against "monopoly" and railroad practices that they thought inhibited economic development. They were not hostile to the factory and corporation as such; and faced with the continuing need for outside capital, and with the complexity and difficulty of corporate regulation, they gradually turned their attention in the direction of good government and public services. In their zeal for efficiency and expansion, in fact, the Progressives manifested the principal features of business development itself.

By the 1920s the term *progress* appeared in a subtly different context, associated less with popular crusades than with chambers of commerce and Rotary Clubs. It carried the meaning of efficiency and development rather than of reform. The "progressive" community now was the community that had good government, great churches, improved schools, industry and business, real estate booms, and boosters. "The business class political philosophy of the New South," political scientist H. C. Nixon wrote in 1931, "is broad enough to include programs of highway improvement, educational expansion, and health regulation. But it does not embrace any comprehensive challenge to laissez faire in the sphere of relationship between capital and labor." On the theme of efficiency, Nixon found, "Business methods in government tend to get the right of way over the ideas of checks and balances, and governmental functions tend to expand in response to social or business needs."

It all began to sound like the New South creed warmed over. The fact of the matter is that the fever had never subsided. As Francis B. Simkins pointed out, the New South creed merely adopted education and good roads along with industrial growth to make up the trinity of southern progress.

These developments unfolded along the lines traced in Wiebe's *The Search for Order.* In all the areas of new responsibility the characteristic themes of business progressivism—expansion and efficiency—accompanied a transition from the missionary era to one of bureaucracy and professionalism. The growing functions of public service became the responsibility of permanent agencies —school boards, highway commissions, public and private charities—served by professional staffs and directing programs that emphasized rationalization and orderliness.

These themes manifested themselves, for example, in the southern education movement, culminating in the programs of the General Education Board (GEB), which became after 1902 the great central directorate for the expansion and rationalization of state systems. Nearly every educational innovation of any significance was developed by the GEB. The leaders in the good roads movement pursued similar goals, seeking to develop networks of highways that would follow an overall plan rather than capricious localism. Even farm organizations cultivated "businesslike" procedures and interest-groups politics. All of these things, and many others, exemplified a quest for excellence, a passion for doing things well and in a regular, systematic manner.

In the search for order, society would have to look to its informed element and to professional experts in various fields. But the new élite of talent and achievement, while it was responsible for significant innovations, would not become a dominant élite in the South. The bureaucratic mentality was too ill-suited to the southern temperament—although it could be accommodated so long as it remained a stabilizing influence.

In other ways, progressivism seems clearly to have been the legatee, almost the inevitable corollary of Bourbonism in its more patrician and "responsible" moods. If Progressives took from the Populists their ideas of a more active government, their reforms served mainly the goals of the New South creed and not, incidentally, the self-interest of the New South élite. Education served both the goal of orderly civilization and that of prosperity. The people were poor, school reformer Charles W. Dabney argued, because the schools were poor. Railroad regulation, which probably inspired more passion than anything other than the race question, helped local merchants and shippers as well as farmers. Good roads provided outlets for farm products but also served merchants, industrialists, road builders, truckers, even at first railroads. Land drainage, the most ambitious program of Florida Progressives, benefitted land speculators, opened a new empire of truck farming, and established the winter base for a ragged army of migratory workers. Progressive governors repeatedly engaged in strike-breaking. Good government often meant frugality more than service to the people.

A recent student of progressivism, J. Morgan Kousser, has no doubt overstated the case, but still with some persuasiveness: "If Progressivism had a general theme in the South it was hardly 'democracy' or 'the greatest good for the greatest number,' but the stabilization of society, especially the economy, in the interests of the local established powers, at the expense of the lower strata in the South, and sometimes at the expense of out-of-state corporations. After all, neither group voted in Dixie."

Here we reach the nub of the question, the right to vote, and come face to face with an insistent paradox that historians of the South have never resolved, or for that matter clearly acknowledged. In writing about the political evolution of the New South after the Bourbon era, one dominant theme of historians has been the revolt of the rednecks, the rise of the common man, the growth of white democracy. Because of the common white man's prejudices, however, the rise of white democracy was accompanied by a rapid decline in the status of blacks: disfranchisement, segregation, and proscription. So goes the familiar story of the transition from populism to progressivism. Yet, at one and the same time, the level of participation in elections, by white voters as well as black, declined steadily from the early 1890s, and precipitantly after the turn of the century. Where is the rising white democracy in that? And if it be argued that the decline merely reflects the lessening importance of general elections and the rise of the white primary, there remains the problem that even in the white primaries the levels of participation generally ran well below those that had prevailed in the general elections of the 1880s and early 1890s or which still prevailed in most of the nation.

Contrary to a common impression, the Bourbon era of the 1880s and, in most states, the 1890s, had seen much higher participation, with 60 to 70 percent of the potential voters turning out, white and black. It was, moreover, a time of vigorous party competition in which Republican, Independent, and Populist challengers provided credible alternatives to Democratic hegemony, and occasionally won elections. This was followed after the turn of the century by a sharp drop in electoral participation which left party competition almost nonexistent.

The question of who disfranchised whom in the South

remains in the historiography of the period about as murky as the definition of Bourbon, Populist, or Progressive. Was disfranchisement, after all, the natural outcome of the revolt of the rednecks who, frustrated by poverty and political defeat, turned their aggression upon the relatively helpless blacks? Or was it a deliberate class-conscious effort of Bourbon reactionaries to use the disfranchisement of Negroes as a shield for the simultaneous disfranchisement of poor whites by poll taxes and literacy tests? Or was it, as the Progressives saw it, an enlightened reform to purify the electorate by elimination of the ignorant, vicious, and corruptible elements?

Any serious effort to comprehend the meaning of disfranchisement must, I think, take into account all three of these factors. Clearly after 1896 there did set in among the white farmers a reaction against the halfhearted bi-racial coalitions of the 1890s. But just as clearly this reaction came to serve the purposes of other elements in the community. Aside from Mississippi and South Carolina and Georgia, in fact, it is difficult to find a single state in which farmer leaders assumed important roles in the disfranchisement movement. Even so, the movement in Mississippi had Bourbon support, the author of the disfranchisement provisions in South Carolina's Constitution of 1895 was a conservative Charlestonian, and the chief leader of the movement in Georgia was the Progressive Governor Hoke Smith.

Some new light has been shed into this murky area by J. Morgan Kousser's book, *The Shaping of Southern Politics: Suffrage Restriction and the Establishment of the One-Party South, 1880–1910*. Kousser boldly and persuasively advances the argument that disfranchisement was a deliberate and conscious effort to eliminate from the electorate as many whites of the lower orders as possible. Kousser backs up his argument by evidence that in the late nineteenth century a substantial retreat from the principle of universal male suffrage took place—in the North because of the immigrant vote (although he does not show that the sentiment led to any consequential legislation there) and in the South not just because of black enfranchisement but because of the supposed threat from the ignorant and propertyless in general. All this fits into the mugwump mentality: the urge to good government, which is to say government by the "better class" of people. In this respect southern Bourbons and Progressives were mugwumps as authentically as any gentleman reformers of Boston.

The movement for disfranchisement drew its leaders for the most part from upper-class whites, whether Bourbon or Progressive. There was an easy, indeed almost imperceptible transition from, say, the conservative Edward McCrady of Charleston who in 1882 proposed disfranchising "the dense mass of ignorant voters of both colors," and the Progressive Edgar Gardner Murphy of Montgomery, who in 1907 condemned a suffrage so wide it gave power to the "crudest" classes. The restrictionists, according to Kousser, "claimed that the members of these groups had 'no will of their own,' or were mere 'political automatons,' or were 'corruptible,' when what they really meant was that those voters stubbornly refused to come over to the Democratic side. As a consequence of the lower strata's voting habits, Southern Democrats had to stuff ballot boxes and try to bribe and intimidate voters in order to win elections."

The demoralizing moral effects of such behavior, therefore, made it necessary to deprive black voters of the ballot in order to stop Democrats from stealing their votes. Disfranchisement thus typically became a Progressive reform in the interest of good government. In retrospect the Bourbon system had a certain tone of aristocratic carelessness and toleration that was unacceptable in the new age of efficiency. Where the Bourbons had been content for the most part to let local communities handle the problem, and even to tolerate a degree of black independence, the new policy of statewide regulation to accomplish disfranchisement fitted the Progressive urge to rationalize procedures both political and economic. It had the further merit that, where Bourbons had to count out their opponents, the Progressives simply stopped them from running at all by disfranchising their potential followers. This had the added advantage of quieting criticism of fraud in southern elections, but that had its ironies, too. The fraud was simply transferred from the electoral process to the registration process, by vesting in registrars the right to judge qualifications.

A further irony is the way in which the nature of the Fifteenth Amendment expedited the process of disfranchising poor whites. The frustrated farmers could be mobilized to the support of disfranchising Negroes, but since the Fifteenth Amendment made it impossible to exclude Negroes as such, the available devices, mainly poll taxes and literacy tests, would inexorably catch up large numbers of poor whites in the net. As a consequence, there was bitter opposition from some of the more vigilant leaders of the poor whites—particularly those who clung longest to the People's party, who saw the outcome all too clearly—but the opposition was neutralized by providing loopholes through which white voters could slip. As alternatives to literacy (but not to the poll tax) the new suffrage provisions commonly included grandfather clauses and understanding clauses. What limited evidence we have, however, indicates that few illiterates were willing to undergo the humiliation of appealing to these devices. How many whites were simply permitted to slip the net by indulgent registrars, of course, we cannot tell. One of the more incredible aspects of the whole thing, moreover, was the naivete of Progressive intellectuals, if not Progressive politicos, about the amount of potential fraud built into this "reform": not only the reliance upon the flexible consciences of registrars, who were entrusted with judging qualifications, but the poll tax in the hands of scheming politicians who bought up blocks of poll-tax receipts for use by loyal or purchasable followings.

Whatever the motivations of its authors, the consequence of disfranchisement was to stabilize and secure the Solid South. Paraphrasing Sigmund Freud's remark that in life anatomy is destiny, Richard Goodwin has written that in government structure is policy. If this is true, the structure of the southern electorate insured a policy of class distinctions. The rigid solidarity of the South, according to a common and persistent opinion, downgraded issues and programs, encouraged a politics of personalities, gave rise to demagogues, fostered neglect and nonvoting, and reduced the region's influence in both national parties.

Paradoxically, the solidarity of the one-party system brought a fragmentation of the political process into shifting and ephemeral personal factions. "Such extremely disorganized political systems," according to J. Morgan Kousser, "generally reward elites, who can translate their superior social and economic positions into political power to gain what they desire or at least block what they strongly oppose; whereas, members of the lower strata, lacking comparable resources, require collective organization if they are to assert themselves."

Habits of deference continued to prevail. By the 1920s the old country gentleman may have faded into memory, but it was a memory kept perpetually green in the myth of the Old South. In his place had risen the type that political scientist Jasper Shannon called the "county-seat élites," or the "banker-merchant-farmer-lawyer-doctor governing class," and what Ralph McGill called "a certain type, small-town rich man." This village nabob may not have been the stuff of which historical romance is made, but his authority in the community at least equaled if it did not exceed that of the storied aristocrat. The South "more than any other part of the country, retains the idea of the Gentry versus the Lower Classes," Sinclair Lewis wrote in 1929 after visiting the scene of the strike at Marion, North Carolina. "It doesn't take much to feel that you are in the Gentry. Owning a small grocery . . . will do it." In the New South, as in the Old, one did not have to share the power of the élite in order to share the mystique.

One of the neglected areas of recent southern history, George Mowry said in *Another Look at the Twentieth-Century South*, is this persistent "élite and its relationship to the area's politicians." Even such an expert on southern politics as V. O. Key, Jr., Mowry noted, had to be equivocal on the subject for want of clear knowledge: "The South," Key wrote, "*may* have a relatively small economic elite that possesses high cohesion." The results of the existing system, however, were more certain: "a social and economic structure in which the gulf between the rich and the poor has been extraordinarily wide."

It was a power that had an impact on national as well as local policy. In *The South and the Concurrent Majority*, David Potter, with his rare gift for bringing new perspectives into focus, argued that John C. Calhoun's theory of the concurrent majority expressed the essence of a negative power which the South maintained for nearly a century after his death. Calhoun simply failed to anticipate, and in fact rejected, the means: "zealous, even fanatical adherence to one political party." Instead of Calhoun's fine-spun theory of a dual executive, or any other formalistic contrivance, the effective devices were the seniority system and the power of congressional committees supplemented by complex rules of procedure, the party caucus, unlimited discussion in the Senate, and the two-thirds rule in Democratic conventions.

The record, Mowry said, "is written in beating back the twin threats of liberal or progressive state governments and of labor unions, in maintaining the wage differentials between classes within the South, and by comparison to those existing elsewhere in the nation, and in holding to a minimum federal intervention in either the industrial or the race question"—at least for a long time. And the two questions were connected: "Sustained racial passions meant one-party government, one-party government meant upper-class control, and hence antiunion government, Q. E. D.: a certain level of racial animosity worked to the benefit of the owning classes."

The first serious threat to the traditional structure came, ironically, from the national Democratic party to which southern politicians had held with such tenacious loyalty—and by way of intervention in both the industrial and race questions. The programs of the New Deal, designed to meet the problems of depression, almost inadvertently jeopardized the traditional power structure which rested on the control of property, labor, credit, and local government. Relief projects reduced dependency; labor standards raised wages; farm programs upset landlord-tenant relationships; government credit bypassed bankers; new federal programs skirted country commissioners and sometimes even state agencies. The trends became more ominous in 1935, when the "Second New Deal" swung from recovery to reform with such measures as WPA, social security, the Wagner Labor Relations Act, the "soak-the-rich" tax, and later, the Farm Tenant and Housing Acts of 1937 and the Fair Labor Standards Act of 1938. What is more, the political necessities of the New Deal thrust northern democrats into alliance with organized labor and the black voters while southern liberals dreamed of reviving the Populist coalition in the South itself. In 1937 a simmering rebellion of southern Democrats broke into open revolt on the issue of reforming the Supreme Court, and since that time reaction against the policies of the national Democratic party has repeatedly disrupted southern democracy and led to the renewal of the Republican party within the region.

But all that is another story. To follow this disruption of the Solid South in detail would stretch the length of these remarks beyond the limits of patience. Suffice it to repeat the point made at the outset: that the region seems to have passed a major watershed in recent years, with the disappearance of so many old landmarks—the one-party system, the one-crop system in agriculture and industry, the death of Jim Crow, the rise in levels of education. With the rise of a two-party system, southern politics seem headed toward a more structured framework than in the past, with an electorate, now unburdened of the old restrictions, drawn into greater participation by party competition. The new situation would seem to open southern politics to a wider range of possibilities than ever before. No doubt there will be some surprises ahead. One of them may be the persistence of tradition, the persistence of the old sense of community if not of the old habits of deference.